Field Work

Field Work

Seamus Heaney

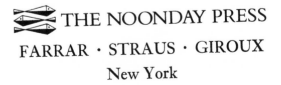
THE NOONDAY PRESS
FARRAR · STRAUS · GIROUX
New York

for Karl and Jane Miller

Copyright © 1976, 1979 by Seamus Heaney
All rights reserved
First published in 1979 by Faber and Faber Limited
First American printing, 1979
Printed in the United States of America
Library of Congress Cataloging in Publication Data
Heaney, Seamus.   Field work.   I. Title.
PR6058.E2F5   1979   821'.9'14   79-20556
Noonday Press edition, 1989
Twelfth printing, 1995

Contents

Acknowledgements

Acknowledgements are due to the editors of the following where some of these poems appeared for the first time: *Antaeus, Ciphers, Encounter, Honest Ulsterman, The Irish Press, The Irish Times, The Listener, Little Word Machine, Mars, The New Review, The New Yorker, The New York Review of Books, The Paris Review, Poetry Now* (BBC Radio), *Poetry Wales, Prospice, Sewanee Review, Thames Poetry, Threshold* and *The Times Literary Supplement.*

The quotation from Dante, *Purgatorio*, used in *The Strand at Lough Beg*, is taken from the Penguin translation by Dorothy L. Sayers (1955).

Elegy and *Leavings* appeared in a limited edition from Deerfield Press. *Glanmore Sonnets* were published by Charles Seluzicki under the title *Hedge School* (Janus Press).

Oysters

Our shells clacked on the plates.
My tongue was a filling estuary,
My palate hung with starlight:
As I tasted the salty Pleiades
Orion dipped his foot into the water.

Alive and violated
They lay on their beds of ice:
Bivalves: the split bulb
And philandering sigh of ocean.
Millions of them ripped and shucked and scattered.

We had driven to that coast
Through flowers and limestone
And there we were, toasting friendship,
Laying down a perfect memory
In the cool of thatch and crockery.

Over the Alps, packed deep in hay and snow,
The Romans hauled their oysters south to Rome:
I saw damp panniers disgorge
The frond-lipped, brine-stung
Glut of privilege

And was angry that my trust could not repose
In the clear light, like poetry or freedom
Leaning in from sea. I ate the day
Deliberately, that its tang
Might quicken me all into verb, pure verb.

Triptych

I

After a Killing

There they were, as if our memory hatched them,
As if the unquiet founders walked again:
Two young men with rifles on the hill,
Profane and bracing as their instruments.

Who's sorry for our trouble?
Who dreamt that we might dwell among ourselves
In rain and scoured light and wind-dried stones?
Basalt, blood, water, headstones, leeches.

In that neuter original loneliness
From Brandon to Dunseverick
I think of small-eyed survivor flowers,
The pined-for, unmolested orchid.

I see a stone house by a pier.
Elbow room. Broad window light.
The heart lifts. You walk twenty yards
To the boats and buy mackerel.

And to-day a girl walks in home to us
Carrying a basket full of new potatoes,
Three tight green cabbages, and carrots
With the tops and mould still fresh on them.

II

Sibyl

My tongue moved, a swung relaxing hinge.
I said to her, 'What will become of us?'
And as forgotten water in a well might shake
At an explosion under morning

Or a crack run up a gable,
She began to speak.
'I think our very form is bound to change.
Dogs in a siege. Saurian relapses. Pismires.

Unless forgiveness finds its nerve and voice,
Unless the helmeted and bleeding tree
Can green and open buds like infants' fists
And the fouled magma incubate

Bright nymphs. . . . My people think money
And talk weather. Oil-rigs lull their future
On single acquisitive stems. Silence
Has shoaled into the trawlers' echo-sounders.

The ground we kept our ear to for so long
Is flayed or calloused, and its entrails
Tented by an impious augury.
Our island is full of comfortless noises.'

III

At the Water's Edge

On Devenish I heard a snipe
And the keeper's recital of elegies
Under the tower. Carved monastic heads
Were crumbling like bread on water.

On Boa the god-eyed, sex-mouthed stone
Socketed between graves, two-faced, trepanned,
Answered my silence with silence.
A stoup for rain water. Anathema.

From a cold hearthstone on Horse Island
I watched the sky beyond the open chimney
And listened to the thick rotations
Of an army helicopter patrolling.

A hammer and a cracked jug full of cobwebs
Lay on the windowsill. Everything in me
Wanted to bow down, to offer up,
To go barefoot, foetal and penitential,

And pray at the water's edge.
How we crept before we walked! I remembered
The helicopter shadowing our march at Newry,
The scared, irrevocable steps.

The Toome Road

One morning early I met armoured cars
In convoy, warbling along on powerful tyres,
All camouflaged with broken alder branches,
And headphoned soldiers standing up in turrets.
How long were they approaching down my roads
As if they owned them? The whole country was sleeping.
I had rights-of-way, fields, cattle in my keeping,
Tractors hitched to buckrakes in open sheds,
Silos, chill gates, wet slates, the greens and reds
Of outhouse roofs. Whom should I run to tell
Among all of those with their back doors on the latch
For the bringer of bad news, that small-hours visitant
Who, by being expected, might be kept distant?
Sowers of seed, erectors of headstones . . .
O charioteers, above your dormant guns,
It stands here still, stands vibrant as you pass,
The invisible, untoppled omphalos.

A Drink of Water

She came every morning to draw water
Like an old bat staggering up the field:
The pump's whooping cough, the bucket's clatter
And slow diminuendo as it filled,
Announced her. I recall
Her grey apron, the pocked white enamel
Of the brimming bucket, and the treble
Creak of her voice like the pump's handle.
Nights when a full moon lifted past her gable
It fell back through her window and would lie
Into the water set out on the table.
Where I have dipped to drink again, to be
Faithful to the admonishment on her cup,
Remember the Giver fading off the lip.

The Strand at Lough Beg

IN MEMORY OF COLUM MCCARTNEY

> All round this little island, on the strand
> Far down below there, where the breakers strive,
> Grow the tall rushes from the oozy sand.
> > Dante, *Purgatorio*, I, 100–103

Leaving the white glow of filling stations
And a few lonely streetlamps among fields
You climbed the hills towards Newtownhamilton
Past the Fews Forest, out beneath the stars—
Along that road, a high, bare pilgrim's track
Where Sweeney fled before the bloodied heads,
Goat-beards and dogs' eyes in a demon pack
Blazing out of the ground, snapping and squealing.
What blazed ahead of you? A faked road block?
The red lamp swung, the sudden brakes and stalling
Engine, voices, heads hooded and the cold-nosed gun?
Or in your driving mirror, tailing headlights
That pulled out suddenly and flagged you down
Where you weren't known and far from what you knew:
The lowland clays and waters of Lough Beg,
Church Island's spire, its soft treeline of yew.

There you used hear guns fired behind the house
Long before rising time, when duck shooters
Haunted the marigolds and bulrushes,
But still were scared to find spent cartridges,
Acrid, brassy, genital, ejected,
On your way across the strand to fetch the cows.
For you and yours and yours and mine fought shy,
Spoke an old language of conspirators
And could not crack the whip or seize the day:
Big-voiced scullions, herders, feelers round
Haycocks and hindquarters, talkers in byres,
Slow arbitrators of the burial ground.

Across that strand of yours the cattle graze
Up to their bellies in an early mist
And now they turn their unbewildered gaze
To where we work our way through squeaking sedge
Drowning in dew. Like a dull blade with its edge
Honed bright, Lough Beg half shines under the haze.
I turn because the sweeping of your feet
Has stopped behind me, to find you on your knees
With blood and roadside muck in your hair and eyes,
Then kneel in front of you in brimming grass
And gather up cold handfuls of the dew
To wash you, cousin. I dab you clean with moss
Fine as the drizzle out of a low cloud.
I lift you under the arms and lay you flat.
With rushes that shoot green again, I plait
Green scapulars to wear over your shroud.

A Postcard from North Antrim

IN MEMORY OF SEAN ARMSTRONG

A lone figure is waving
From the thin line of a bridge
Of ropes and slats, slung
Dangerously out between
The cliff-top and the pillar rock.
A nineteenth-century wind.
Dulse-pickers. Sea campions.

A postcard for you, Sean,
And that's you, swinging alone,
Antic, half-afraid,
In your gallowglass's beard
And swallow-tail of serge:
The Carrick-a-Rede Rope Bridge
Ghost-written on sepia.

Or should it be your houseboat
Ethnically furnished,
Redolent of grass?
Should we discover you
Beside those warm-planked, democratic wharves
Among the twilights and guitars
Of Sausalito?

Drop-out on a come-back,
Prince of no-man's land
With your head in clouds or sand,
You were the clown
Social worker of the town
Until your candid forehead stopped
A pointblank teatime bullet.

19

Get up from your blood on the floor.
Here's another boat
In grass by the lough shore,
Turf smoke, a wired hen-run—
Your local, hoped for, unfound commune.
Now recite me *William Bloat*,
Sing of *the Calabar*

Or of Henry Joy McCracken
Who kissed his Mary Ann
On the gallows at Cornmarket.
Or Ballycastle Fair.
'Give us the raw bar!'
'Sing it by brute force
If you forget the air.'

Yet something in your voice
Stayed nearly shut.
Your voice was a harassed pulpit
Leading the melody
It kept at bay,
It was independent, rattling, non-transcendent
Ulster—old decency

And Old Bushmills,
Soda farls, strong tea,
New rope, rock salt, kale plants,
Potato-bread and Woodbine.
Wind through the concrete vents
Of a border check-point.
Cold zinc nailed for a peace line.

Fifteen years ago, come this October,
Crowded on your floor,
I got my arm round Marie's shoulder
For the first time.
'Oh, Sir Jasper, do not touch me!'
You roared across at me,
Chorus-leading, splashing out the wine.

Casualty

I

He would drink by himself
And raise a weathered thumb
Towards the high shelf,
Calling another rum
And blackcurrant, without
Having to raise his voice,
Or order a quick stout
By a lifting of the eyes
And a discreet dumb-show
Of pulling off the top;
At closing time would go
In waders and peaked cap
Into the showery dark,
A dole-kept breadwinner
But a natural for work.
I loved his whole manner,
Sure-footed but too sly,
His deadpan sidling tact,
His fisherman's quick eye
And turned observant back.

Incomprehensible
To him, my other life.
Sometimes, on his high stool,
Too busy with his knife
At a tobacco plug
And not meeting my eye,
In the pause after a slug
He mentioned poetry.
We would be on our own
And, always politic
And shy of condescension,
I would manage by some trick
To switch the talk to eels

Or lore of the horse and cart
Or the Provisionals.

But my tentative art
His turned back watches too:
He was blown to bits
Out drinking in a curfew
Others obeyed, three nights
After they shot dead
The thirteen men in Derry.
PARAS THIRTEEN, the walls said,
BOGSIDE NIL. That Wednesday
Everybody held
His breath and trembled.

II

It was a day of cold
Raw silence, wind-blown
Surplice and soutane:
Rained-on, flower-laden
Coffin after coffin
Seemed to float from the door
Of the packed cathedral
Like blossoms on slow water.
The common funeral
Unrolled its swaddling band,
Lapping, tightening
Till we were braced and bound
Like brothers in a ring.

But he would not be held
At home by his own crowd
Whatever threats were phoned,
Whatever black flags waved.
I see him as he turned
In that bombed offending place,
Remorse fused with terror

In his still knowable face,
His cornered outfaced stare
Blinding in the flash.

He had gone miles away
For he drank like a fish
Nightly, naturally
Swimming towards the lure
Of warm lit-up places,
The blurred mesh and murmur
Drifting among glasses
In the gregarious smoke.
How culpable was he
That last night when he broke
Our tribe's complicity?
'Now you're supposed to be
An educated man,'
I hear him say. 'Puzzle me
The right answer to that one.'

III

I missed his funeral,
Those quiet walkers
And sideways talkers
Shoaling out of his lane
To the respectable
Purring of the hearse . . .
They move in equal pace
With the habitual
Slow consolation
Of a dawdling engine,
The line lifted, hand
Over fist, cold sunshine
On the water, the land
Banked under fog: that morning
I was taken in his boat,
The screw purling, turning

Indolent fathoms white,
I tasted freedom with him.
To get out early, haul
Steadily off the bottom,
Dispraise the catch, and smile
As you find a rhythm
Working you, slow mile by mile,
Into your proper haunt
Somewhere, well out, beyond . . .

Dawn-sniffing revenant,
Plodder through midnight rain,
Question me again.

The Badgers

When the badger glimmered away
into another garden
you stood, half-lit with whiskey,
sensing you had disturbed
some soft returning.

The murdered dead,
you thought.
But could it not have been
some violent shattered boy
nosing out what got mislaid
between the cradle and the explosion,
evenings when windows stood open
and the compost smoked down the backs?

Visitations are taken for signs.
At a second house I listened
for duntings under the laurels
and heard intimations whispered
about being vaguely honoured.

And to read even by carcasses
the badgers have come back.
One that grew notorious
lay untouched in the roadside.
Last night one had me braking
but more in fear than in honour.

Cool from the sett and redolent
of his runs under the night,
the bogey of fern country
broke cover in me
for what he is:
pig family
and not at all what he's painted.

How perilous is it to choose
not to love the life we're shown?
His sturdy dirty body
and interloping grovel.
The intelligence in his bone.
The unquestionable houseboy's shoulders
that could have been my own.

The Singer's House

When they said *Carrickfergus* I could hear
the frosty echo of saltminers' picks.
I imagined it, chambered and glinting,
a township built of light.

What do we say any more
to conjure the salt of our earth?
So much comes and is gone
that should be crystal and kept

and amicable weathers
that bring up the grain of things,
their tang of season and store,
are all the packing we'll get.

So I say to myself *Gweebarra*
and its music hits off the place
like water hitting off granite.
I see the glittering sound

framed in your window,
knives and forks set on oilcloth,
and the seals' heads, suddenly outlined,
scanning everything.

People here used to believe
that drowned souls lived in the seals.
At spring tides they might change shape.
They loved music and swam in for a singer

who might stand at the end of summer
in the mouth of a whitewashed turf-shed,
his shoulder to the jamb, his song
a rowboat far out in evening.

When I came here first you were always singing,
a hint of the clip of the pick
in your winnowing climb and attack.
Raise it again, man. We still believe what we hear.

The Guttural Muse

Late summer, and at midnight
I smelt the heat of the day:
At my window over the hotel car park
I breathed the muddied night airs off the lake
And watched a young crowd leave the discotheque.

Their voices rose up thick and comforting
As oily bubbles the feeding tench sent up
That evening at dusk—the slimy tench
Once called the 'doctor fish' because his slime
Was said to heal the wounds of fish that touched it.

A girl in a white dress
Was being courted out among the cars:
As her voice swarmed and puddled into laughs
I felt like some old pike all badged with sores
Wanting to swim in touch with soft-mouthed life.

In Memoriam Sean O'Riada

He conducted the Ulster Orchestra
like a drover with an ashplant
herding them south.
I watched him from behind,

springy, formally suited,
a black stiletto trembling in its mark,
a quill flourishing itself,
a quickened, whitened head.

'How do you work?
Sometimes I just lie out
like ballast in the bottom of the boat
listening to the cuckoo.'

The gunwale's lifting ear—
trusting the gift,
risking gift's undertow—
is unmanned now

but one whole afternoon
it was deep in both our weights.
We sat awkward on the thwarts
taking turns to cast or row

until mackerel shoaled from under
like a conjured retinue
fawning upon our lures.
He had the *sprezzatura*,

more falconer than fisherman, I'd say,
unhooding a sceptic eye
to greet the mackerel's barred cold,
to pry whatever the cuckoo called.

As he stepped and stooped to the keyboard
he was our jacobite,
he was our young pretender
who marched along the deep

plumed in slow airs and grace notes.
O gannet smacking through scales!
Minnow of light.
Wader of assonance.

Elegy

The way we are living,
timorous or bold,
will have been our life.
Robert Lowell,

the sill geranium is lit
by the lamp I write by,
a wind from the Irish Sea
is shaking it—

here where we all sat
ten days ago, with you,
the master elegist
and welder of English.

As you swayed the talk
and rode on the swaying tiller
of yourself, ribbing me
about my fear of water,

what was not within your empery?
You drank America
like the heart's
iron vodka,

promulgating art's
deliberate, peremptory
love and arrogance.
Your eyes saw what your hand did

as you Englished Russian,
as you bullied out
heart-hammering blank sonnets
of love for Harriet

and Lizzie, and the briny
water-breaking dolphin—
your dorsal nib
gifted at last

to inveigle and to plash,
helmsman, netsman, *retiarius*.
That hand. Warding and grooming
and amphibious.

Two a.m., seaboard weather.
Not the proud sail of your great verse . . .
No. You were our night ferry
thudding in a big sea,

the whole craft ringing
with an armourer's music
the course set wilfully across
the ungovernable and dangerous.

And now a teem of rain
and the geranium *tremens*.
A father's no shield
for his child—

you found the child in me
when you took farewells
under the full bay tree
by the gate in Glanmore,

opulent and restorative
as that lingering summertime,
the fish-dart of your eyes
risking, 'I'll pray for you.'

Glanmore Sonnets

FOR ANN SADDLEMEYER
our heartiest welcomer

I

Vowels ploughed into other: opened ground.
The mildest February for twenty years
Is mist bands over furrows, a deep no sound
Vulnerable to distant gargling tractors.
Our road is steaming, the turned-up acres breathe.
Now the good life could be to cross a field
And art a paradigm of earth new from the lathe
Of ploughs. My lea is deeply tilled.
Old ploughsocks gorge the subsoil of each sense
And I am quickened with a redolence
Of the fundamental dark unblown rose.
Wait then . . . Breasting the mist, in sowers' aprons,
My ghosts come striding into their spring stations.
The dream grain whirls like freakish Easter snows.

II

Sensings, mountings from the hiding places,
Words entering almost the sense of touch
Ferreting themselves out of their dark hutch—
'These things are not secrets but mysteries,'
Oisin Kelly told me years ago
In Belfast, hankering after stone
That connived with the chisel, as if the grain
Remembered what the mallet tapped to know.
Then I landed in the hedge-school of Glanmore
And from the backs of ditches hoped to raise
A voice caught back off slug-horn and slow chanter
That might continue, hold, dispel, appease:
Vowels ploughed into other, opened ground,
Each verse returning like the plough turned round.

III

This evening the cuckoo and the corncrake
(So much, too much) consorted at twilight.
It was all crepuscular and iambic.
Out on the field a baby rabbit
Took his bearings, and I knew the deer
(I've seen them too from the window of the house,
Like connoisseurs, inquisitive of air)
Were careful under larch and May-green spruce.
I had said earlier, 'I won't relapse
From this strange loneliness I've brought us to.
Dorothy and William—' She interrupts:
'You're not going to compare us two . . .?'
Outside a rustling and twig-combing breeze
Refreshes and relents. Is cadences.

IV

I used to lie with an ear to the line
For that way, they said, there should come a sound
Escaping ahead, an iron tune
Of flange and piston pitched along the ground,
But I never heard that. Always, instead,
Struck couplings and shuntings two miles away
Lifted over the woods. The head
Of a horse swirled back from a gate, a grey
Turnover of haunch and mane, and I'd look
Up to the cutting where she'd soon appear.
Two fields back, in the house, small ripples shook
Silently across our drinking water
(As they are shaking now across my heart)
And vanished into where they seemed to start.

V

Soft corrugations in the boortree's trunk,
Its green young shoots, its rods like freckled solder:
It was our bower as children, a greenish, dank
And snapping memory as I get older.
And elderberry I have learned to call it.
I love its blooms like saucers brimmed with meal,
Its berries a swart caviar of shot,
A buoyant spawn, a light bruised out of purple.
Elderberry? It is shires dreaming wine.
Boortree is bower tree, where I played 'touching tongues'
And felt another's texture quick on mine.
So, etymologist of roots and graftings,
I fall back to my tree-house and would crouch
Where small buds shoot and flourish in the hush.

VI

He lived there in the unsayable lights.
He saw the fuchsia in a drizzling noon,
The elderflower at dusk like a risen moon
And green fields greying on the windswept heights.
'I will break through,' he said, 'what I glazed over
With perfect mist and peaceful absences. . . .'
Sudden and sure as the man who dared the ice
And raced his bike across the Moyola River.
A man we never saw. But in that winter
Of nineteen forty-seven, when the snow
Kept the country bright as a studio,
In a cold where things might crystallize or founder,
His story quickened us, a wild white goose
Heard after dark above the drifted house.

VII

Dogger, Rockall, Malin, Irish Sea:
Green, swift upsurges, North Atlantic flux
Conjured by that strong gale-warning voice
Collapse into a sibilant penumbra.
Midnight and closedown. Sirens of the tundra,
Of eel-road, seal-road, keel-road, whale-road, raise
Their wind-compounded keen behind the baize
And drive the trawlers to the lee of Wicklow.
L'Etoile, *Le Guillemot*, *La Belle Hélène*
Nursed their bright names this morning in the bay
That toiled like mortar. It was marvellous
And actual, I said out loud, 'A haven,'
The word deepening, clearing, like the sky
Elsewhere on Minches, Cromarty, The Faroes.

VIII

Thunderlight on the split logs: big raindrops
At body heat and lush with omen
Spattering dark on the hatchet iron.
This morning when a magpie with jerky steps
Inspected a horse asleep beside the wood
I thought of dew on armour and carrion.
What would I meet, blood-boltered, on the road?
How deep into the woodpile sat the toad?
What welters through this dark hush on the crops?
Do you remember that pension in *Les Landes*
Where the old one rocked and rocked and rocked
A mongol in her lap, to little songs?
Come to me quick, I am upstairs shaking.
My all of you birchwood in lightning.

IX

Outside the kitchen window a black rat
Sways on the briar like infected fruit:
'It looked me through, it stared me out, I'm not
Imagining things. Go you out to it.'
Did we come to the wilderness for this?
We have our burnished bay tree at the gate,
Classical, hung with the reek of silage
From the next farm, tart-leafed as inwit.
Blood on a pitch-fork, blood on chaff and hay,
Rats speared in the sweat and dust of threshing—
What is my apology for poetry?
The empty briar is swishing
When I come down, and beyond, your face
Haunts like a new moon glimpsed through tangled glass.

X

I dreamt we slept in a moss in Donegal
On turf banks under blankets, with our faces
Exposed all night in a wetting drizzle,
Pallid as the dripping sapling birches.
Lorenzo and Jessica in a cold climate.
Diarmuid and Grainne waiting to be found.
Darkly asperged and censed, we were laid out
Like breathing effigies on a raised ground.
And in that dream I dreamt—how like you this?—
Our first night years ago in that hotel
When you came with your deliberate kiss
To raise us towards the lovely and painful
Covenants of flesh; our separateness;
The respite in our dewy dreaming faces.

September Song

In the middle of the way
under the wet of late September
the ash tree flails,
our dog is tearing earth beside the house.

In rising ditches the fern subsides.
Rain-logged berries and stones
are rained upon, acorns
shine from grassy verges every morning.

And it's nearly over,
our four years in the hedge-school.
If nobody is going to resin a bow
and test the grieving registers for joy

we might as well put on our old record
of John Field's *Nocturnes*—
his gifts, waste, solitude, reputation, laughter,
all 'Dead in Moscow',

all those gallons of wash for the pure drop,
notes 'like raindrops, pearls on velvet.'
Remember our American wake?
When we first got footloose

they lifted the roof for us in Belfast,
Hammond, Gunn and McAloon
in full cry till the dawn chorus,
insouciant and purposeful.

Gusts, barking, power-lines shaken
and the music wavering. Inside and out,
babes-in-the-wood weather. We toe the line
between the tree in leaf and the bare tree.

An Afterwards

She would plunge all poets in the ninth circle
And fix them, tooth in skull, tonguing for brain;
For backbiting in life she'd make their hell
A rabid egotistical daisy-chain.

Unyielding, spurred, ambitious, unblunted,
Lockjawed, mantrapped, each a fastened badger
Jockeying for position, hasped and mounted
Like Ugolino on Archbishop Roger.

And when she'd make her circuit of the ice,
Aided and abetted by Virgil's wife,
I would cry out, 'My sweet, who wears the bays
In our green land above, whose is the life

Most dedicated and exemplary?'
And she: 'I have closed my widowed ears
To the sulphurous news of poets and poetry.
Why could you not have, oftener, in our years

Unclenched, and come down laughing from your room
And walked the twilight with me and your children—
Like that one evening of elder bloom
And hay, when the wild roses were fading?'

And (as some maker gaffs me in the neck)
'You weren't the worst. You aspired to a kind,
Indifferent, faults-on-both-sides tact.
You left us first, and then those books, behind.'

High Summer

The child cried inconsolably at night.
Because his curls were long and fair
the neighbours called him *la petite*
and listened to him harrowing the air
that damped their roof-tiles and their vines.
At five o'clock, when the landlord's tractor,
familiar, ignorant and hard,
battled and gargled in the yard,
we relished daylight in the shutter
and fell asleep.
                    Slubbed with eddies,
the laden silent river
ran mud and olive into summer.
Swallows mazed from nests caked up on roof-tiles
in the barn: the double doors stood open,
the carter passed ahead of his bowed oxen.

I bought the maggots in paper bags, like sweets,
and fished at evening in the earthy heat
and green reek of the maize.
From that screened bank, as from a plaited frieze,
bamboo rods stuck leniently out,
nodding and waiting, feelers into quiet.
Snails in the grass, bat-squeak, the darkening trees. . . .

'Christopher is teething and cries at night.
But this barn is an ideal place to write:
bare stone, old harness, ledges, shelves, the smell
of hay and silage. Just now, all's hot and still.
I've scattered twenty francs on fishing tackle.'

On the last day, when I was clearing up,
on a warm ledge I found a bag of maggots
and opened it. A black
and throbbing swarm came riddling out

like newsreel of a police force run amok,
sunspotting flies in gauzy meaty flight,
the barristers and black berets of light.

We left by the high bare roads of the *pays basque*
where calvaries sentry the crossroads like masts
and slept that night near goatbells in the mists.

The Otter

When you plunged
The light of Tuscany wavered
And swung through the pool
From top to bottom.

I loved your wet head and smashing crawl,
Your fine swimmer's back and shoulders
Surfacing and surfacing again
This year and every year since.

I sat dry-throated on the warm stones.
You were beyond me.
The mellowed clarities, the grape-deep air
Thinned and disappointed.

Thank God for the slow loadening,
When I hold you now
We are close and deep
As the atmosphere on water.

My two hands are plumbed water.
You are my palpable, lithe
Otter of memory
In the pool of the moment,

Turning to swim on your back,
Each silent, thigh-shaking kick
Re-tilting the light,
Heaving the cool at your neck.

And suddenly you're out,
Back again, intent as ever,
Heavy and frisky in your freshened pelt,
Printing the stones.

The Skunk

Up, black, striped and damasked like the chasuble
At a funeral mass, the skunk's tail
Paraded the skunk. Night after night
I expected her like a visitor.

The refrigerator whinnied into silence.
My desk light softened beyond the verandah.
Small oranges loomed in the orange tree.
I began to be tense as a voyeur.

After eleven years I was composing
Love-letters again, broaching the word 'wife'
Like a stored cask, as if its slender vowel
Had mutated into the night earth and air

Of California. The beautiful, useless
Tang of eucalyptus spelt your absence.
The aftermath of a mouthful of wine
Was like inhaling you off a cold pillow.

And there she was, the intent and glamorous,
Ordinary, mysterious skunk,
Mythologized, demythologized,
Snuffing the boards five feet beyond me.

It all came back to me last night, stirred
By the sootfall of your things at bedtime,
Your head-down, tail-up hunt in a bottom drawer
For the black plunge-line nightdress.

Homecomings

I

Fetch me the sandmartin
skimming and veering
breast to breast with himself
in the clouds in the river.

II

At the worn mouth of the hole
flight after flight after flight
the swoop of his wings
gloved and kissed home.

III

A glottal stillness. An eardrum.
Far in, featherbrains tucked in silence,
a silence of water
lipping the bank.

IV

Mould my shoulders inward to you.
Occlude me.
Be damp clay pouting.
Let me listen under your eaves.

A Dream of Jealousy

Walking with you and another lady
In wooded parkland, the whispering grass
Ran its fingers through our guessing silence
And the trees opened into a shady
Unexpected clearing where we sat down.
I think the candour of the light dismayed us.
We talked about desire and being jealous,
Our conversation a loose single gown
Or a white picnic tablecloth spread out
Like a book of manners in the wilderness.
'Show me,' I said to our companion, 'what
I have much coveted, your breast's mauve star.'
And she consented. O neither these verses
Nor my prudence, love, can heal your wounded stare.

Polder

After the sudden outburst and the squalls
I hooped you with my arms

and remembered that what could be contained
inside this caliper embrace

the Dutch called *bosom*; and *fathom*
what the extended arms took in.

I have reclaimed my polder,
all its salty grass and mud-slick banks;

under fathoms of air, like an old willow
I stir a little on my creel of roots.

Field Work

I

Where the sally tree went pale in every breeze,
where the perfect eye of the nesting blackbird watched,
where one fern was always green

I was standing watching you
take the pad from the gatehouse at the crossing
and reach to lift a white wash off the whins.

I could see the vaccination mark
stretched on your upper arm, and smell the coal smell
of the train that comes between us, a slow goods,

waggon after waggon full of big-eyed cattle.

II

But your vaccination mark is on your thigh,
an O that's healed into the bark.

Except a dryad's not a woman
you are my wounded dryad

in a mothering smell of wet
and ring-wormed chestnuts.

Our moon was small and far,
was a coin long gazed at

brilliant on the *Pequod*'s mast
across Atlantic and Pacific waters.

Not the mud slick,
not the black weedy water
full of alder cones and pock-marked leaves.

Not the cow parsley in winter
with its old whitened shins and wrists,
its sibilance, its shaking.

Not even the tart green shade of summer
thick with butterflies
and fungus plump as a leather saddle.

No. But in a still corner,
braced to its pebble-dashed wall,
heavy, earth-drawn, all mouth and eye,

the sunflower, dreaming umber.

IV

Catspiss smell,
the pink bloom open:
I press a leaf
of the flowering currant
on the back of your hand
for the tight slow burn
of its sticky juice
to prime your skin,
and your veins to be crossed
criss-cross with leaf-veins.
I lick my thumb
and dip it in mould,
I anoint the anointed
leaf-shape. Mould
blooms and pigments
the back of your hand
like a birthmark—
my umber one,
you are stained, stained
to perfection.

Song

A rowan like a lipsticked girl.
Between the by-road and the main road
Alder trees at a wet and dripping distance
Stand off among the rushes.

There are the mud-flowers of dialect
And the immortelles of perfect pitch
And that moment when the bird sings very close
To the music of what happens.

Leavings

A soft whoosh, the sunset blaze
of straw on blackened stubble,
a thatch-deep, freshening
barbarous crimson burn—

I rode down England
as they fired the crop
that was the leavings of a crop,
the smashed tow-coloured barley,

down from Ely's Lady Chapel,
the sweet tenor latin
forever banished,
the sumptuous windows

threshed clear by Thomas Cromwell.
Which circle does he tread,
scalding on cobbles,
each one a broken statue's head?

After midnight, after summer,
to walk in a sparking field,
to smell dew and ashes
and start Will Brangwen's ghost

from the hot soot—
a breaking sheaf of light,
abroad in the hiss
and clash of stooking.

The Harvest Bow

As you plaited the harvest bow
You implicated the mellowed silence in you
In wheat that does not rust
But brightens as it tightens twist by twist
Into a knowable corona,
A throwaway love-knot of straw.

Hands that aged round ashplants and cane sticks
And lapped the spurs on a lifetime of game cocks
Harked to their gift and worked with fine intent
Until your fingers moved somnambulant:
I tell and finger it like braille,
Gleaning the unsaid off the palpable,

And if I spy into its golden loops
I see us walk between the railway slopes
Into an evening of long grass and midges,
Blue smoke straight up, old beds and ploughs in hedges,
An auction notice on an outhouse wall—
You with a harvest bow in your lapel,

Me with the fishing rod, already homesick
For the big lift of these evenings, as your stick
Whacking the tips off weeds and bushes
Beats out of time, and beats, but flushes
Nothing: that original townland
Still tongue-tied in the straw tied by your hand.

The end of art is peace
Could be the motto of this frail device
That I have pinned up on our deal dresser—
Like a drawn snare
Slipped lately by the spirit of the corn
Yet burnished by its passage, and still warm.

In Memoriam Francis Ledwidge

KILLED IN FRANCE 31 JULY 1917

The bronze soldier hitches a bronze cape
That crumples stiffly in imagined wind
No matter how the real winds buff and sweep
His sudden hunkering run, forever craned

Over Flanders. Helmet and haversack,
The gun's firm slope from butt to bayonet,
The loyal, fallen names on the embossed plaque—
It all meant little to the worried pet

I was in nineteen forty-six or seven,
Gripping my Aunt Mary by the hand
Along the Portstewart prom, then round the crescent
To thread the Castle Walk out to the strand.

The pilot from Coleraine sailed to the coal-boat.
Courting couples rose out of the scooped dunes.
A farmer stripped to his studs and shiny waistcoat
Rolled the trousers down on his timid shins.

At night when coloured bulbs strung out the sea-front
Country voices rose from a cliff-top shelter
With news of a great litter—'We'll pet the runt!'—
And barbed wire that had torn a friesian's elder.

Francis Ledwidge, you courted at the seaside
Beyond Drogheda one Sunday afternoon.
Literary, sweet-talking, countrified,
You pedalled out the leafy road from Slane

Where you belonged, among the dolorous
And lovely: the May altar of wild flowers,
Easter water sprinkled in outhouses,
Mass-rocks and hill-top raths and raftered byres.

59

I think of you in your Tommy's uniform,
A haunted Catholic face, pallid and brave,
Ghosting the trenches with a bloom of hawthorn
Or silence cored from a Boyne passage-grave.

It's summer, nineteen-fifteen. I see the girl
My aunt was then, herding on the long acre.
Behind a low bush in the Dardanelles
You suck stones to make your dry mouth water.

It's nineteen-seventeen. She still herds cows
But a big strafe puts the candles out in Ypres:
'My soul is by the Boyne, cutting new meadows. . . .
My country wears her confirmation dress.'

'To be called a British soldier while my country
Has no place among nations. . . .' You were rent
By shrapnel six weeks later. 'I am sorry
That party politics should divide our tents.'

In you, our dead enigma, all the strains
Criss-cross in useless equilibrium
And as the wind tunes through this vigilant bronze
I hear again the sure confusing drum

You followed from Boyne water to the Balkans
But miss the twilit note your flute should sound.
You were not keyed or pitched like these true-blue ones
Though all of you consort now underground.

Ugolino

We had already left him. I walked the ice
And saw two soldered in a frozen hole
On top of other, one's skull capping the other's,
Gnawing at him where the neck and head
Are grafted to the sweet fruit of the brain,
Like a famine victim at a loaf of bread.
So the berserk Tydeus gnashed and fed
Upon the severed head of Menalippus
As if it were some spattered carnal melon.
'You,' I shouted, 'you on top, what hate
Makes you so ravenous and insatiable?
What keeps you so monstrously at rut?
Is there any story I can tell
For you, in the world above, against him?
If my tongue by then's not withered in my throat
I will report the truth and clear your name.'

That sinner eased his mouth up off his meal
To answer me, and wiped it with the hair
Left growing on his victim's ravaged skull,
Then said, 'Even before I speak
The thought of having to relive all that
Desperate time makes my heart sick;
Yet while I weep to say them, I would sow
My words like curses—that they might increase
And multiply upon this head I gnaw.
I know you come from Florence by your accent
But I have no idea who you are
Nor how you ever managed your descent.
Still, you should know my name, for I was Count
Ugolino, this was Archbishop Roger,
And why I act the jockey to his mount
Is surely common knowledge; how my good faith
Was easy prey to his malignancy,

How I was taken, held, and put to death.
But you must hear something you cannot know
If you're to judge him—the cruelty
Of my death at his hands. So listen now.

Others will pine as I pined in that jail
Which is called Hunger after me, and watch
As I watched through a narrow hole
Moon after moon, bright and somnambulant,
Pass overhead, until that night I dreamt
The bad dream and my future's veil was rent.
I saw a wolf-hunt: this man rode the hill
Between Pisa and Lucca, hounding down
The wolf and wolf-cubs. He was lordly and masterful,
His pack in keen condition, his company
Deployed ahead of him, Gualandi
And Sismundi as well, and Lanfranchi,
Who soon wore down wolf-father and wolf-sons
And my hallucination
Was all sharp teeth and bleeding flanks ripped open.
When I awoke before the dawn, my head
Swam with cries of my sons who slept in tears
Beside me there, crying out for bread.
(If your sympathy has not already started
At all that my heart was foresuffering
And if you are not crying, you are hardhearted.)

They were awake now, it was near the time
For food to be brought in as usual,
Each one of them disturbed after his dream,
When I heard the door being nailed and hammered
Shut, far down in the nightmare tower.
I stared in my sons' faces and spoke no word.
My eyes were dry and my heart was stony.
They cried and my little Anselm said,
"What's wrong? Why are you staring, daddy?"

But I shed no tears, I made no reply
All through that day, all through the night that followed
Until another sun blushed in the sky
And sent a small beam probing the distress
Inside those prison walls. Then when I saw
The image of my face in their four faces
I bit on my two hands in desperation
And they, since they thought hunger drove me to it,
Rose up suddenly in agitation
Saying, "Father, it will greatly ease our pain
If you eat us instead, and you who dressed us
In this sad flesh undress us here again."
So then I calmed myself to keep them calm.
We hushed. That day and the next stole past us
And earth seemed hardened against me and them.
For four days we let the silence gather.
Then, throwing himself flat in front of me,
Gaddo said, "Why don't you help me, father?"
He died like that, and surely as you see
Me here, one by one I saw my three
Drop dead during the fifth day and the sixth day
Until I saw no more. Searching, blinded,
For two days I groped over them and called them.
Then hunger killed where grief had only wounded.'
When he had said all this, his eyes rolled
And his teeth, like a dog's teeth clamping round a bone,
Bit into the skull and again took hold.

Pisa! Pisa, your sounds are like a hiss
Sizzling in our country's grassy language.
And since the neighbour states have been remiss
In your extermination, let a huge
Dyke of islands bar the Arno's mouth, let
Capraia and Gorgona dam and deluge
You and your population. For the sins
Of Ugolino, who betrayed your forts,
Should never have been visited on his sons.

Your atrocity was Theban. They were young
And innocent: Hugh and Brigata
And the other two whose names are in my song.

from Dante, *Inferno*, xxxii *and* xxxiii

Notes

Triptych

I. Brandon is on the south-western coast of Ireland, in Co. Kerry; Dunseverick is in the north-east, in Co. Antrim.

III. Devenish, Boa and Horse Island are all islands in Lough Erne in Co. Fernanaugh.

The march at Newry took place in 1972, a week after Bloody Sunday.

The Strand at Lough Beg

Colum McCartney, a relative of the author's, was the victim of a random sectarian killing in the late summer of 1975.

Sweeney is the hero of a Middle Irish prose and poem sequence, one part of which takes place in the Fews in Co. Arnagh.

A Postcard from North Antrim

Sean Armstrong, a native of North Antrim, lived for a while in Sausalito, California, before returning to Belfast in the early seventies.

The Carrick-a-Rede Rope Bridge was a celebrated tourist attraction on the northern Irish coast.

"William Bloat," "The Cruise of the Calabar," "Henry Joy" and "Ballycastle Fair" are Ulster songs and recitations.

Woodbine was a common brand of cigarette.

The Singer's House

There are salt-mines at the town of Carrickfergus in Co. Antrim.

Gweebarra is the name of a river and a bay in Co. Donegal.

In Memoriam: Sean O'Riada

Sean O'Riada (1931–1971) was an influential composer, and the moving force in the revival of Irish music over the past two decades.

Glanmore Sonnets

Glanmore, in Co. Wicklow, was the author's home for four years after he left Belfast in 1972.

V. "Boortree" is Ulster dialect for the elder tree, and probably derives from the Scots pronunciation of "bower tree."

X. Diarmuid and Grainne are fugitive lovers of Irish legend.

September Song

John Field, the Irish composer and originator of the nocturne, is buried under a headstone that reads: "John Field/Born in Ireland/in 1782./Dead in Moscow/in 1837."

In Memoriam: Francis Ledwidge

Francis Ledwidge (1891–1917) was friendly with some of the leaders of the 1916 Rising yet, like thousands of other Irishmen of the time, felt himself constrained to enlist in the British Army to defend "the rights of small nations."